THE ONE PRAYER
EVERYONE
NEEDS TO KNOW

THE ONE PRAYER EVERYONE NEEDS TO KNOW

RITA HORSTMAN

The One Prayer Everyone Needs to Know
Copyright © 2019 by Rita Horstman. All rights reserved.

No part of this publication may be reproduced, stored in a retrieval system or transmitted in any way by any means, electronic, mechanical, photocopy, recording or otherwise without the prior permission of the author except as provided by USA copyright law.

The opinions expressed by the author are not necessarily those of URLink Print and Media.

1603 Capitol Ave., Suite 310 Cheyenne, Wyoming USA 82001
1-888-980-6523 | admin@urlinkpublishing.com

URLink Print and Media is committed to excellence in the publishing industry.

Book design copyright © 2019 by URLink Print and Media. All rights reserved.

Published in the United States of America

ISBN 978-1-64367-645-6 (Paperback)
ISBN 978-1-64367-644-9 (Digital)

18.07.19

CONTENTS

Foreword 7
Chapter One 9
Chapter Two 11
Chapter Three 12
Chapter Four 13
Chapter Five 14
Chapter Six 15
Chapter Seven 16
Chapter Eight 17
Chapter Nine 18
Chapter Ten 19
Chapter Eleven 20

FOREWORD

Many people through their lifetimes on this earth struggle with the reason; the reason we are here, their purpose, their ultimate goal, and meaning in life. This book explores those often-unspoken questions through Scripture and personal reflection, providing comfort and inspiration through struggles and events that can challenge any person's beliefs, heart, and faith. It also shares a brief instruction to embark on an opportunity to grow our character in today's broken world.

CHAPTER ONE

The Reason, Our Mission, Our Purpose, Our Goal

Scripturally, through all my endeavors and life challenges, I have learned to take solace in the one prayer Christ taught us to pray...

> *Our Father, who art in heaven, hallowed be thy name, thy kingdom come, thy will be done on earth as it is in heaven. Give us this day our daily bread, and forgive us for our trespasses as we forgive those who trespass against us, lead us not into temptation, but deliver us from evil, for thine is the kingdom, the power, and the glory forever.*
>
> *Matthew 6:9-13*

This divine prayer and literal instruction for life is quoted in the Gospel as the prayer Jesus taught us to pray. So, we have our instruction, our mission, our purpose, right? All we need is given in this very important prayer, right? Our manual, our instructions, our goals for life?

Yes. Divine instruction is in the often-quoted Gospel prayer; however, we forget to compare, to review, to relive, and to renew!

Each line of the prayer offers important instructions. If we review the prayer carefully, line-by-line, we will find the inspiration we need to overcome life's struggles. Following, I will briefly describe the message contained in each line of the prayer. I will explore each line in more depth in the chapters that remain and offer some questions for personal reflection.

Hallowed be thy name: Respect is displayed in the prayer and should be displayed to our God (our God, who came in human form through the image of Christ, our perfect example for how to live on this earth).

Thy kingdom come: We do not have heaven on earth yet, but this is our goal and our promise, our hope and our mission for making this earth a better place every day.

Thy will be done: God is good all the time and always wants what is best for you!

Give us this day our daily bread: Provide for our needs today—spiritual, mental, physical, and emotional.

Forgive us our trespasses as we forgive those who trespass against us: We don't have complete heaven here yet; forgiveness and grace are required for us and for others.

Lead us not into temptation: We live in a fallen world, again, not heaven on earth yet. Please give us the will to withstand temptation, to model your sacrifice and your love. With your help all things are possible. Only with God can we get through it!

Deliver us from evil: When we fall or when others make us fall, save us, pick us up, help us learn, and help us move on.

For thine is the kingdom, the power, and the glory forever: We strive to be with You, to do good, to love as You love us. Only your kingdom is what we shall strive for; the Universal Church, in Christ, with all glory to You, not us!

CHAPTER TWO

Hallowed be Thy Name: Respect is displayed in the prayer and should be displayed to our God (our God, who came in human form through the image of Christ, our perfect example for how to live on this earth).

What better example can we have than God in human form? Jesus led the perfect life, fulfilling His mission to show us how to live and to show us His love. How can we not respect the true Father, teacher, pastor, and friend? Because we are all human and imperfect, we need our leader to help us grow.

When we learn to respect Him through our blessings and our trials and tribulations, we grow in our blessings and in our character. By displaying respect, attending church out of respect, joining in fellowship with others, and following His examples, we can grow personally and enjoy more passionately the blessings He gives to us.

It is not always easy to understand how adversity can help us grow. It is during these adverse times we sometimes lose sight of our true blessings and Savior. However, it is through knowing His continued presence in all our situations that we can become even closer to Him.

Respect is synonymous with love. We are asked to love God and love others as ourselves. May we passionately seek to respect and love God in all we do and all we are. May we use our gifts and talents to be blessings to Him, to ourselves, and others. Lord, hallowed be Your name!

CHAPTER THREE

Thy Kingdom Come: We do not have heaven on earth yet, but this is our goal and our promise, our hope and our mission for making this earth a better place every day.

This verse is a reminder that we do not have heaven on earth yet, but that it is always in the works! Thy Kingdom Come is like the Great Commission that was given to all the disciples: "Go and baptize the nations making disciples" (Matthew 28:19). Nations refers to "people" and discipline comes from the word disciple. If we make an effort to discipline ourselves, teaching ourselves, it is less difficult to witness to someone else.

Remembering Christ-like examples and even starting with the Golden Rule can be an awesome way to make disciples of other people. Leading by example, as we are led by Christ's examples, is important.

It helps to remember while in trials, we have an imperfect world. Thy Kingdom Come helps us understand why we still have imperfection. We can live above it and respond to trials in a Christian way. Jesus reminds us not to worry. When we have trials and burdens, it is nice to take refuge in the fact that we are all a work in progress. One day, we will no longer have trials or tribulations, but until then, use the solid rock we have, our friend in Jesus, and take all our trials to Him in prayer. Thy Kingdom come!

How do you see your purpose in developing God's Kingdom? What can or do you already do each day to move God's Kingdom forward?

CHAPTER FOUR

Thy Will be Done: God is good all the time and always wants what is best for you!

 God's will is His choice. Although we are given free will, we don't always make the best or right decisions. This is part of our growing process. God knows and has a perfect will. What He wants is what is always best, and when we lean on His understanding and not our own, we find peace in how things can work out. Again, we can use the song, "What a Friend we have in Jesus," everything to God in prayer.

 When we submit our will and ourselves to Him, He can lead and direct our lives. We aren't perfect and may fall, but He will help lead, guide, and direct us back into His will for our lives. His purpose is what matters and what is best. We can take comfort in knowing that when we are God-led we are safe. Thy will be done!

 How do you submit to God's will in your life?

CHAPTER FIVE

Give us this Day our Daily Bread: Provide for our needs today—spiritual, mental, physical, and emotional.

Health is based on a balance of all needs. Humans need bread or manna spiritually, mentally, physically, and emotionally. Asking for assistance from God for our needs is humble and wise. He knows our needs better than we do.

Thank you, Father, for providing for our needs. Lead us to ask you for specific, defined needs and fill the gaps when we are unable to define them. Thank you for the opportunity to come to you for health and for all needs. Give us this day our daily bread!

Whose health do you need to pray for?

List things that you need God to assist you with.

Thank God for providing for your needs. Specifically list the needs that God has met.

Also, create a page for needs you still have that God will meet in the future.

CHAPTER SIX

Forgive us Our Trespasses as We Forgive Those Who Trespass Against Us: We don't have compete heaven here yet; forgiveness and grace are required for us and for others.

Help us forgive others so we too can be forgiven. Forgiveness is a pardon for actions and hurts, the refusal to hold someone guilty beyond what they are accountable. Forgiveness doesn't mean we forget all accountability. (The Bible does outline one sin that is unforgiveable, blasphemy, and I do not want to undermine that clear warning.) There may be some restitution that needs to be paid by the debtor, but forgiveness and grace is then letting go and loving that person as deeply, or even more deeply than before.

Recognizing that we need God's grace helps us to extend that same grace to others. Forgiveness of ourselves and of others is ongoing. Because we are imperfect, we have to move forward grudge-free, loving others and letting go.

Thank you, Father, for forgiveness!

Who in your life do you need to forgive? Maybe yourself or someone else? Why do you need to forgive them, and how can you pray about it to help you with forgiveness?

How will you move forward to extend God's grace and forgiveness to those you have forgiven? List some ways you will show that grace.

CHAPTER SEVEN

Lead Us not into Temptation: We live in a fallen world, again, not heaven on earth yet. Please give us the will to withstand temptation, to model your sacrifice and your love. With your help all things are possible. Only with God can we get through it!

Jesus was tempted many times, but was the only perfect human to withstand temptation and live a perfect life. He taught us this prayer to withstand temptation only with His help and through prayer. When we withstand temptation, a better result waits for us and we grow in our character.

He knows we can be weak, but He is strong. He is with us and has lived in this world to teach us how to try and live. We may sometimes waiver and fall, but by His grace we can also be saved and get back up again.

Lord, help us withstand temptations in Your power with all glory to You. Lead us in a righteous path!

What do you find tempting and how can you pray about it or remove yourself from that temptation?

CHAPTER EIGHT

Deliver Us from Evil: When we fall, or others make us fall, save us, pick us up, help us learn, and help us move on.

When this fallen world lies heavy upon us, help us to rise above it. A good friend always gave advice from her mother: "When stress comes, don't get under it, stay on top of it." That is how life can get, only sometimes we are "under it" before we know it. That is why Jesus gave us a prayer to protect us.

Because this world is fallen, we can always use extra guidance. The Lord's Prayer continually guides us and watches out for us. God is our Savior and our protector.

Father, help us when life overwhelms us. Protect us always.

Can you think of a time you have fallen and God has saved you? Recall that experience, write about it, and journal about the faith that prevailed to bring you out of that situation.

CHAPTER NINE

For Thine is the Kingdom, The Power, and The Glory Forever: We strive to be with You, to do good, to love as You love us. Only Your kingdom is what we shall strive for; the Universal Church, in Christ, with all Glory to You, not us!

It is so good to always see the whole forest through the trees. Keeping our end in mind is so important. God's kingdom is what we should always strive for. A friend once said we can either build the kingdom of God up or we can tear it down; we can build people up or we can tear them down.

Building up our neighbors blesses God's kingdom and brings glory to Him. Living in harmony, addressing others in love, and living the best we can also brings glory to God. Take each day starting out with God's kingdom in mind. It makes our big problems seem smaller.

Help us, Lord, to put Your Kingdom first and may we always give praise and glory to You.

Can you recall a time you praised God for good things in your life? Write about that experience and about how you plan to give praise in the future.

CHAPTER TEN

Holding on to the Prayer and Building Our Faith.

Jesus said if we have faith as big as a mustard seed, we can move mountains, so why do we falter? We have our prayer, our mission, our understanding; what gets in the way? (Matthew 13: 31-32)

Have you ever struggled personally with questions and answers to trials in life? Do life events, deaths, illnesses, and pain make us shake and question our faith? Do we lean on God for understanding without questioning His unconditional love? Jesus does love us unconditionally, just like the song, "Jesus Loves Me, This I know." How often do we forget that pure and simple meaning from our childhood songs?

We do have a challenge and a purpose, and we do have to try. When this fallen world shows us pain, we must always hold onto our hope and turn to God for help and understanding, ultimately clinging to His mission and His purposes in our minds.

I have personally shared questions, through pain, illness, and family loss, and have only been able to move forward by clinging to our prayer, the Lord's Prayer, that He gave with our perfect mission and purpose in life. We can pray to hold onto the hope, the promise, and live to fulfill the mission, while overcoming our troubles each day.

How can the Lord's Prayer help you move past a difficult time? What can you remember about the Lord's prayer to help you live a better future?

CHAPTER ELEVEN

Living for the Reason, the Purpose, Our Mission! Your Kingdom Come!

Grow your character? Be big-picture thinkers, conquer our pain with and through Him, and get up and move forward again? You have got to be kidding me! The Lord's Prayer, although Divine, cannot be that simple. Life cannot be simple. Yet, Christ said we must become like little children to enter the Kingdom of Heaven (Matthew 18:2-6).

We can feel touches of His Kingdom every day, through the unconditional love and trust put into practice as a child does. Putting our faith in Jesus Christ, not experiences, not words, not pain, but in Him to grow and move past our fears, our pain, and cling to hope through Him, gives us freedom to move forward again.

Anyone who has experienced child birth knows its tremendous physical and emotional pain, yet what we are given through perseverance is a blessing beyond our control. I like to think of this earth as going through many birthing pains, yet our blessing, and the best, is yet to come.

Prayer for Closing:

Help us, Lord, to pray Your prayer with understanding, perseverance, guidance, and hope. Direct us every day to live for You, and become the people You want us to be. Thank You for Your love,

In Jesus Christ's name,

Amen

www.ingramcontent.com/pod-product-compliance
Lightning Source LLC
LaVergne TN
LVHW021751060526
838200LV00052B/3578